NEIGHBORHOOD HELPERS

Veterinarians

BY CECILIA MINDEN

The Child's World

Content Adviser:
Stuart Porter, DVM, Program
Director and Professor of
Veterinary Technology, Blue
Ridge Community College,
Weyers Cave, Virginia

Published in the United States of America by The Child's World®
PO Box 326
Chanhassen, MN 55317-0326
800-599-READ
www.childsworld.com

Acknowledgements

The Child's World®: Mary Berendes, Publishing Director

Editorial Directions, Inc.: E. Russell Primm, Editorial Director; Katie Marsico, Managing Editor and Line Editor; Judith Shiffer, Assistant Editor; Caroline Wood, Editorial Assistant; Susan Hindman, Copy Editor; Wendy Mead, Proofreader; Mike Helenthal, Rory Mabin, and Caroline Wood, Fact Checkers; Tim Griffin/IndexServ, Indexer; Cian Loughlin O'Day, Photo Researcher; Linda S. Koutris, Photo Selector

The Design Lab: Kathleen Petelinsek, Design and Art Production

Photographs ©: Cover: left—Comstock Images, right/frontispiece—Photodisc/Getty Images. Interior: 4, 16, 17—Photodisc/Getty Images; 5, 11—RubberBall Productions; 7—Chip Simons/Taxi/ Getty Images; 8-9—LWA/JDC/Corbis; 10-11—Reuters/Corbis; 12—Robin Murphy; 14-15—Homer Sykes/Alamy Images; 19—Bo Jansson/pixonnet.com/Alamy Images; 20—Jim Craigmyle/Corbis; 22-23—Kaz Mori/The Image Bank/Getty Images; 24—Coneyl Jay/Stone/Getty Images; 26-27—Larry Williams & Associates/zefa/Corbis; 29—Rebecca Emery/Taxi/Getty Images.

Library of Congress Cataloging-in-Publication Data

Minden, Cecilia.
  Veterinarians / by Cecilia Minden.
    p. cm. — (Neighborhood helpers)
  ISBN 1-59296-571-7 (library bound : alk. paper)
  1. Veterinarians—Juvenile literature. 2. Veterinary medicine—Juvenile literature. I. Title. II. Series.
  SF756.M57 2006
  636.089'0695—dc22   2005026224

NEIGHBORHOOD HELPERS

TABLE OF CONTENTS

Sarah

Hello. My name is Sarah. Many people live and work in my neighborhood. Each of them helps the neighborhood in different ways.

I thought of all the things I like to do. I like animals. I help take care of the pets in our house.

How could I help my neighborhood when I grow up?

The first school of veterinary medicine opened in 1762 in Lyons, France. The first U.S. veterinary school opened one hundred years later.

I COULD BE A VETERINARIAN!

Veterinarians are doctors who work with animals. Animals can't tell the doctor what is hurting. A veterinarian has to put together different pieces of information to figure out what is wrong.

The best part of being a veterinarian is working with animals all day long!

Kids who enjoy helping animals might make good veterinarians. Veterinarians need to be very patient and gentle.

LEARN ABOUT THIS NEIGHBORHOOD HELPER!

The best way to learn is to ask questions. Words such as *who, what, where, when,* and *why* will help me learn about being a veterinarian.

Asking a veterinarian questions will help you learn more about his job.

Where Can I Learn More?

American Veterinary
Medical Association
1931 N. Meacham Road
Suite 100
Schaumburg, IL 60173

Association of
American Veterinary
Medical Colleges
1101 Vermont Avenue NW
Suite 301
Washington, DC 20005

WHO CAN BECOME A VETERINARIAN?

Boys and girls who are good with animals may want to become veterinarians. It is also important for veterinarians to be gentle and to have a lot of patience. They have to handle nervous or sick animals. They often must speak to worried owners.

Veterinarians help the neighborhood in many ways. Some provide care

Veterinarians help both zoo animals and family pets.

for family pets. Others examine farm animals, wildlife, and zoo animals.

MEET A VETERINARIAN!

This is Dr. Robin Downing. Dr. Robin is a veterinarian in Windsor, Colorado. When she is not at her hospital, she likes to travel all over the world teaching people how to care for animals.

Dr. Robin loves helping people learn how to care for animals.

How Many Veterinarians Are There?

About 58,000 people work as veterinarians.

WHERE CAN I LEARN TO BE A VETERINARIAN?

It takes a long time to become a veterinarian. Students go to a school of veterinary medicine for four years after they graduate from college. Veterinarians can choose to specialize, which means they learn a lot about one thing in particular. A veterinarian may want to work with only one animal family such as horses or pigs. Dr. Robin treats family pets such as dogs, cats, rabbits, rats, ferrets, and guinea pigs.

Veterinarians who specialize treat only certain types of animals.

How Much School Will I Need?

Many students in veterinary school already have a four-year college degree. Most veterinary schools require at least two years of college courses. Veterinary school takes four years. Veterinarians must pass tests given by the state where they live. They are then given a license so they can work.

WHAT DOES A VETERINARIAN NEED TO DO HER JOB?

Dr. Robin uses many different instruments to take care of her animals. Many of these instruments are like the ones doctors use to take care of people! Dr. Robin uses a stethoscope to listen to an animal's heart, an otoscope to look in its ears, and an ophthalmoscope to look in its eyes.

Dr. Robin uses a **microscope.** Sometimes she does a blood test on

microscope (MYE-kruh-skope) an instrument with powerful lenses that allows scientists to study very tiny objects

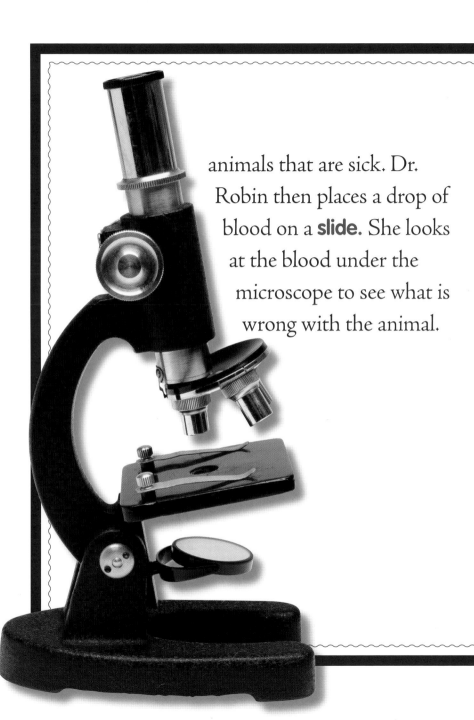

animals that are sick. Dr. Robin then places a drop of blood on a **slide.** She looks at the blood under the microscope to see what is wrong with the animal.

slide (SLYDE) a small piece of glass that is used to view objects under a microscope

WHERE DOES A VETERINARIAN WORK?

Dr. Robin works in a hospital that looks just like a hospital for humans. The only difference is that Dr. Robin's hospital is much smaller. There are exam rooms for the animals, a **laboratory** for testing blood and urine, and a **pharmacy.** There is also a surgery suite for animals that need an operation.

There are two kinds of workdays

Most veterinarians treat animals in an exam room.

at Dr. Robin's hospital. Some days are outpatient days. Animals, or patients, come in for a visit but then go home the same day. An owner might bring a pet in for a checkup or to make sure it is getting the right medicine. Maybe the patient isn't feeling well and the owner wants the veterinarian to figure out what is wrong.

Sometimes people bring their pets to the veterinarian for an outpatient visit.

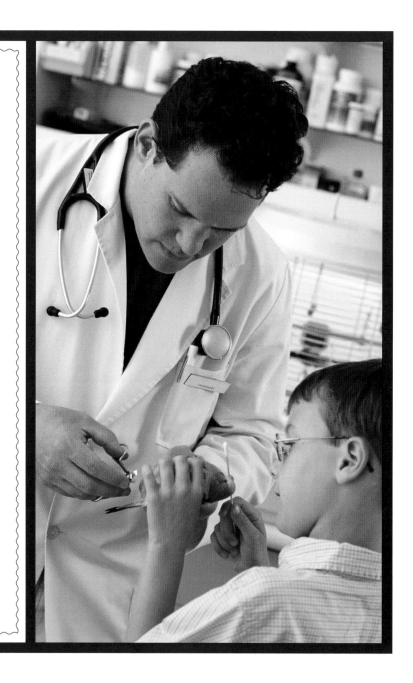

There are also workdays when surgery is performed. This is when Dr. Robin treats animals that need an operation. An owner usually arrives early in the morning and drops her pet off at the hospital. Dr. Robin and her staff check to make sure the patient is well enough to have the surgery. The animal is then given medicine so it doesn't feel any pain. Dr. Robin keeps a close eye on the patient after the surgery. She wants to make sure the animal is recovering well. The owner can usually come back for her pet the next day.

How Much Money Will I Make?

Most veterinarians make between $50,000 and $86,000 a year.

WHO WORKS WITH VETERINARIANS?

There are many people who help Dr. Robin care for animals. A receptionist greets each owner and patient. A veterinary nurse and a veterinary technician assist Dr. Robin with medical care.

Nurses and technicians help veterinarians care for patients.

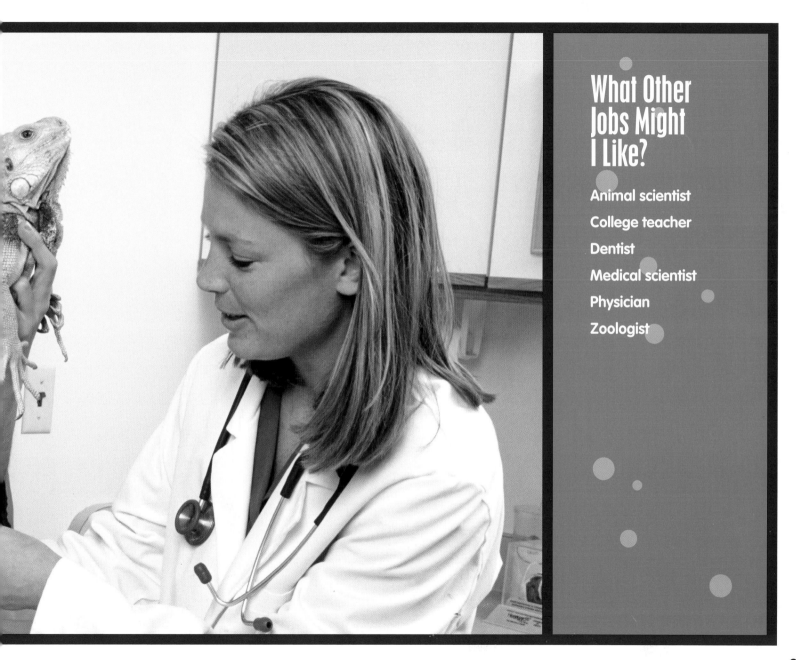

What Other Jobs Might I Like?

Animal scientist

College teacher

Dentist

Medical scientist

Physician

Zoologist

WHEN IS A VETERINARIAN AN ESCAPE ARTIST?

Dr. Robin once had a patient with a very unusual dog collar. This curious puppy had gotten her head stuck in a cement block. Dr. Robin and her staff gave the puppy some medicine to calm her down. They gently pushed and pulled until the puppy's head was free.

Sometimes veterinarians rescue animals in emergency situations. Veterinarians are always working hard to protect animals and keep them healthy.

How Might My Job Change?

Most veterinarians start off working for other veterinarians. They eventually gain experience, and many go on to open their own veterinary offices. Some veterinarians even become teachers in colleges of veterinary medicine.

I WANT TO BE A VETERINARIAN!

I think being a veterinarian would be a great way to be a neighborhood helper. Someday I may be the doctor you see at the animal hospital!

Good dog! Maybe one day you'll be taking care of the pets in your neighborhood.

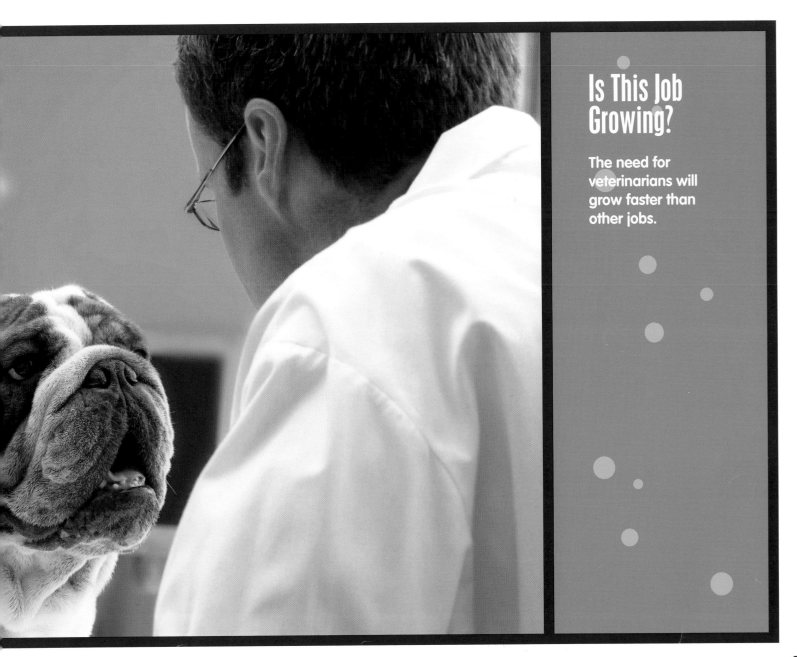

Is This Job Growing?

The need for veterinarians will grow faster than other jobs.

WHY DON'T YOU TRY BEING A VETERINARIAN?

Do you think you would like to be a veterinarian? Why don't you try giving your pet a daily massage? Start at your pet's head. Slowly and gently work your hands all the way to the tail. A massage will help you build a bond with your animal friend. Your hands will help you learn what your animal feels like. You should tell your veterinarian right away if you find a lump or bump that doesn't feel right!

Massage is good for animals and will help you learn about your pet's body.

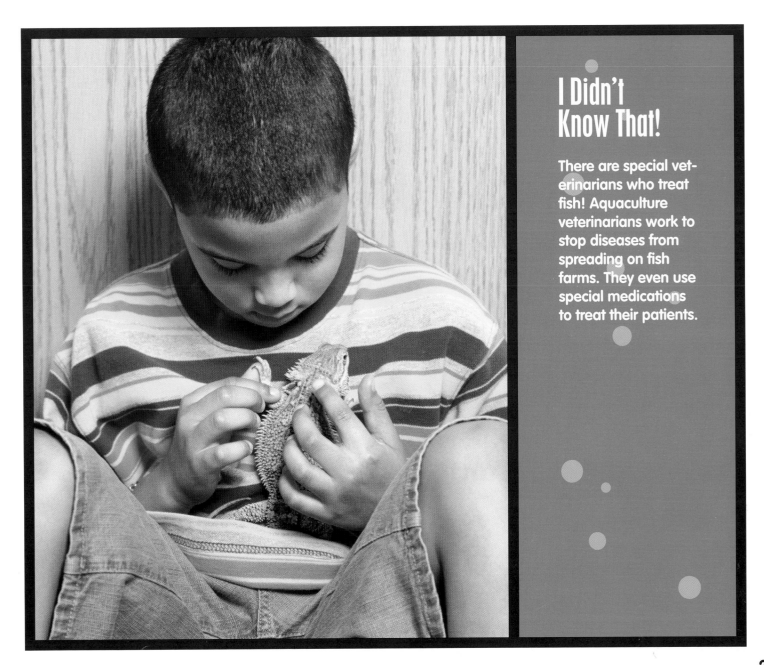

I Didn't Know That!

There are special veterinarians who treat fish! Aquaculture veterinarians work to stop diseases from spreading on fish farms. They even use special medications to treat their patients.

HOW TO LEARN MORE ABOUT VETERINARIANS

BOOKS

Bowman-Kruhm, Mary. *A Day in the Life of a Veterinarian*. New York: PowerKids Press, 2000.

Englart, Mindi Rose. *Veterinarian*. San Diego: Blackbirch Press, 2003.

Kalman, Bobbie. *Veterinarians Help Keep Animals Healthy*. New York: Crabtree Publishing, 2005.

Miller, Heather. *Veterinarian*. Chicago: Heinemann Library, 2003.

Parks, Peggy. *Veterinarian*. San Diego: Kidhaven Press, 2004.

WEB SITES

Visit our home page for lots of links about veterinarians:
http://www.childsworld.com/links

Note to Parents, Teachers, and Librarians:

We routinely check our Web links to make sure they're safe, active sites—so encourage your readers to check them out!

ABOUT THE AUTHOR:

Dr. Cecilia Minden is a university professor and reading specialist with classroom and administrative experience in grades K–12. She is the author of many books for early readers. Cecilia and her husband Dave Cupp live in North Carolina. She earned her PhD in reading education from the University of Virginia.

INDEX